I Received a Bookmark
From an Angel

I Received a Bookmark From an Angel

Encounters, Legalism, and Spirits That
Roam the Universe!

My Bookmark is Inside the Book.
God's Twelve-Step Program for Dealing with Grief

Julie Ringer

iUniverse, Inc.
Bloomington

I Received a Bookmark From an Angel

Poems by Julie Ringer

Scripture quotations are from the King James and New International versions of the Bible.

iUniverse books may be ordered through booksellers or by contacting:

iUniverse
1663 Liberty Drive
Bloomington, IN 47403
www.iuniverse.com
1-800-Authors (1-800-288-4677)

ISBN: 978-1-4620-2328-8 (sc)
ISBN: 978-1-4620-2329-5 (ebk)

Printed in the United States of America

iUniverse rev. date: 07/21/2011

Contents

The Lord is my inspiration—the one I live for—and I wait for His return. If it wasn't for the Lord, I never would have written this book. He was my inspiration to keep me going during the times when I felt like quitting. It is His blood and the cross that will save everyone from their sins!

Introduction

I always enjoyed reading the Word of God. The craving for wanting to know who He really was has always been inside of me!

In this book, I want to share with you some of my encounters that led me to my bookmark I received from an angel. The encounters that I had through my life and my bookmark that I received are not the reasons I wrote this book. The reason I wrote this book is that I was pressured by the Lord to write about Bondage of Legalism.

The first chapter will take you through a journey from my childhood to my adulthood. Reading my encounters will offer a lot more understanding of how I know my bookmark came from an angel.

The next chapter will take you to the Bondage of Legalism. As you keep reading on, this will take you to different places. Let the Lord lead you to where He wants to take you!

Chapter 1

My Spirit World and Me

The Spirits That Roamed the Night

Growing up, I was raised with three older siblings—two sisters and a brother—so that made me the youngest in the family. We lived in a gigantic eight-bedroom, two-story house. Dad always had renters occupying the second story. My oldest sister had her own bedroom that we affectionately called the "purple room" because not only were the walls painted purple, but she had purple carpeting on the floors as well. When she moved out, it became my room.

I loved my new room—my room that I had all to myself. After a while, things began to happen! There were many nights when I would feel the presence of what seemed like a tremendous amount of evil spirits coming from the thin, long closet. It felt as if they were scrunched up in there like sardines. I could feel them coming out of the closet as I heard their footsteps coming toward me. I felt them swarming around my bed. Whenever I felt

1

the presence of these evil spirits, I would sneak into my parents' bedroom and go to sleep on the floor next to their bed. Sometimes I would lie down right by their doorway. I just could not shake the feeling of these evil spirits. Sometimes I would sleep in another bedroom—that was when I would actually see them. Wide awake in bed, I looked through the living room into the dining room. I was able to catch a glimpse of the spirits that were constantly tormenting me. It was surprising how tall they appeared to be. There was one woman in particular who had long, dark, wavy hair; she was very thin and seemed to be standing in the distance. I saw her at times as she was roaming through the house. I still recall with vivid clarity how she would always slant her head to the left because she was too tall—despite the fact that we had extremely high ceilings. There was also a man who was not quite as tall as she was. These were the two I would see the most at different times of the night. It never really mattered which bedroom I stayed in—I would still hear their footsteps walking through the house. My childhood home was also where I first heard the evil spirits talking. I called it mumbling because I would hear them talking but could not understand what they were saying. It was the mumbling of the evil spirit world.

One night when I was quite young, I spent the night at a friend's house. After everyone was asleep, I began to hear mumbling outside the bedroom window. I knew that it was the mumbling of the evil spirits that I would hear at home. I could hear their footsteps coming up the stairs, so I covered my head with the blankets. After a while, the footsteps stopped. I pulled the covers down just enough to see, but there was nothing except the empty darkness. I pulled the covers up over my head again; the footsteps continued up the stairs, and the mumbling outside the window droned on in the dark stillness of the night. All I heard that night was the mumbling and the footsteps all night long. Up all night! After I left that house, I never thought of sleeping over there again.

There have been several other times that I have heard this horrible demon spirit world mumbling. I have heard that horrible mumbling more than a half-dozen times in my life. Even now, at the house I live in with my husband, there have been times that I've heard the same kind of mumbling outside our bedroom window. As my faith and knowledge in the Lord Jesus Christ has grown stronger, I have learned much more about the spirit world. I have also learned that there is power in the name of Jesus Christ. Since I have learned of the power His name holds, I have found that I am able to rebuke these spirits in His name. "Submit yourselves, then, to God. Resist the devil, and he will flee from you" (James 4:7).

Angel on a Motorcycle

My first relationship with a boy occurred when I was about fourteen years old. Unfortunately, the relationship drew me away from the close relationship I had with

Jesus. I began to lose focus on the things that meant so much to me. I spent a lot of time with my boyfriend, putting Jesus on the back burner while drifting further away from Him. When I was seventeen, I had an experience that I would never forget. My boyfriend and I were riding a motorcycle through town; we stopped at an intersection for a red light. I turned to my left and saw a man on a motorcycle kitty-corner to us. He had black curly hair and a medium build. He was staring intently at me with his eyes wide open. I had never seen eyes like them before; they looked human, but seemed to have a bright pulsating light emanating from them that made them stand out. It was as if he could see right through me. My insides were quaking; I felt as if I had come face to face with God Himself. I kept staring intently at his sharp, piercing eyes because—no matter how hard I tried—I could not keep my eyes from his. Suddenly, he began shouting at me: "Jesus Christ is coming back very, very soon!" Over and over again, he repeated these words with such power and authority in his voice. The light turned green and we took off. My boyfriend asked, "Who was that?" I told him that I had never seen him before in my life. I had no idea who he was. The experience was scary, but I knew he was an angel! As I thought back to what happened, I asked myself why I had been so scared. I can only think that his eye contact was so strong. I felt as if he was literally looking into my soul. I felt that this angel came with a message much deeper than I realized at the time. I was about to make a decision that could change the path of my life. Now that I think back, I was drawing closer to my boyfriend—while I was drawing further away from my relationship with God. I have now come to realize that every decision we make affects our entire life and destiny. Sometimes we make decisions that we want for our life instead of waiting or choosing the steps that are ordered by the Lord for our lives. If you wait on the Lord before making your decisions so that they are ordered by Him, it can save you much unnecessary grief and pain. This is a lesson that I had to learn; it led me to an angel who gave me the bookmark that listed "God's twelve-step program for dealing with grief."

The Fuzzy White Ball

During my first marriage, there was an incident that I can vividly recall even to this day. One night, I was sitting in bed reading my Bible. My husband was sleeping next to me when something across the room caught my attention. It is hard to describe.

What I saw was like a white fuzzy ball. It was so evil that you could feel it. As it was coming toward us, I pushed myself back against the headboard, trying to get away from it. Trembling, I wasn't sure where it was going, but I knew I didn't want it near me. It went past me and right on my husband. He woke up right away! He started screaming and yelling, "Get away, you devil!" He ripped the whole bedroom apart while he was screaming like a madman. After the incident, I was left with a horrible feeling of fear that I couldn't shake. At that time, I knew about Jesus. Now when I think back, I wonder why I didn't rebuke that spirit.

My Trip to Poland

In my mid-twenties—after I had been married for a few years—I began to long very deeply to have a child. I had drawn very close to the Lord. At this time, we were living in a town near Milwaukee called Burlington. This time of my life was spent in constant prayer—talking to Jesus and reading the Bible. Jesus was everything to me—he was my life! One day, I started searching the Scriptures for passages that talked about believing in Jesus, asking for anything you desired, and having your prayers answered. I committed one of scriptures in particular to memory. "And this is the confidence that we have in Him, that if we ask anything according to His will, He hears us; And if we know that He hears us whatsoever we ask, we know that we have the petitions that we desired of Him" (1 John 5:14-15).

I studied many other scriptures as well to help me build my faith. I wanted a set of twins! I went to the Lord in prayer and told him very specifically what I wanted: a boy and a girl around fourteen months old. As I prayed, I told Him exactly what the scriptures had said—that if I would ask in His name, I would receive what I was asking for. I remember telling the Lord that I knew He could hear me and that His word was true. I was claiming His promises as I had been instructed to do—and I believed that He would grant my request.

Afterward, I kept on talking to Jesus. I spent a couple of hours just talking to the Lord. All of a sudden, His presence filled the house with His spirit—I could feel His spirit come through me. He spoke in my spirit, promising me a set of twins. My tears started to flow. His presence stayed with me for many hours after that experience. I was walking on cloud nine! I believed that He would keep His promise—though I had no idea how it would happen. I had no kids—having a baby seemed like an impossible situation. I knew that I would have to wait and be patient. I told everyone about the promise.

Whenever I went back to visit my hometown, I would always attend one church. During one visit, I was telling everyone what the Lord had said to me. My mother was the only person who really believed me. I knew that no one else would believe me, but it was something that I could not keep inside! I knew what the Lord said to me and believed that it would happen.

A few months after that visit, my husband and I decided to adopt. I really thought that this was going to be my promise fulfilled. We decided to adopt from Poland and I started the paperwork. I decided to make a visit to Poland with a few other people who wanted to help me adopt. We checked out all the orphanages. At one of the orphanages, I was shocked to see all the children in dirty diapers. They only changed them once a day—no matter how much the child soiled his or her diaper. After going through all these orphanages, I was told that there was nothing here for me. I stayed for another month before I decided to go back home. I felt defeated because I was hurting. I began to focus on what the Lord had said to me as I drew my strength from His promise. I was really trying to pull myself together and be more patient.

A few months later, I went back to Poland. I'm not sure why I made that decision, but I guess I just felt drawn back to that place. After I arrived, I started checking all the orphanages again, but wherever I went, I was told that there were no children available. At that point, I didn't know what to think anymore!

Being in Poland during those two visits was very difficult for me. It was completely different from the United States. Of course, almost everyone spoke Polish. It was a very unpleasant experience for me. I longed for my comfortable way of life. I was very confused and sad. I wondered what my next action was going to be. I knew that I had to do something quickly. I remember looking up at the sky all the time, wishing I could go back home. I had reached a point where I wanted to give up! I would try to remember what the Lord had said to me. I tried to keep believing as I was holding on to His promise. After some thought, I decided to fast and pray until the Lord fulfilled His promise to me. That is what I did! After ten days of fasting, I was so miserable and hungry that I was about to give up! I knew what the Lord had said, but I was confused and didn't understand. I was in a place where I did not want to be and wondered what I was supposed to do next.

All of a sudden, the phone rang. A person said, "We have a set of twins for you! They are a boy and a girl who were twelve months old." As the call ended, I was very excited. I knew that the person at the other end of the phone could hear the excitement in my voice. I went for a long walk to pray and give thanks to the Lord. I cried many tears of gratitude and joy. I began the process for all the paperwork that was needed to bring my kids home with me. I was in Poland for three months. When I took them home to America, they were fourteen months old. He fulfilled His promise to me—exactly what I had asked for. When I got home, I told everyone the good news about how the Lord had given me the request I asked of Him. Everyone was lost for words, but was happy to welcome home Luke and Lea, who were born in Poland and are now United States citizens.

Another White Fuzzy Ball

The marriage to my first husband did not last. After our divorce, I met my second husband, David. One evening, we decided to go visit his friend, Jeff. As we were sitting at the kitchen table, I looked across the room and saw a white fuzzy ball coming toward me. I could feel inside of me that it was something good. I relaxed and waited for the spirit to come to me. I knew that the Lord had something to say as the spirit went through me. The spirit told me to draw myself closer to Jesus with all my heart. Things were going to happen down the road and I was going to need Him for strength! I had no idea why the spirit came to me at that time. Now I know why!

Where is That Music Coming From?

One evening in bed, I started to hear music that seemingly had no point of origin. It sounded like heavenly music. I could hear many people singing like a magnificent choir. I never cared for choir music, but this music was awesome and truly beautiful. Every time I heard this music, I would search desperately for where it was coming from. I would go through every room in the house, but I would find nothing. I finally realized that the music was coming from within my own head. I thought that I was losing my mind! I would use my hands to shake my head back and forth in an attempt to rid myself of this music. Even though the music was awesome and beautiful, I still wanted it out of my head. It was something unknown to me and I wanted it to go away. I never told anyone because I was afraid that people would think that I was crazy. I started to do a little research about the situation.

In the New Testament, it says there is one family in heaven and earth (Ephesians 3:15). "from whom every family in heaven and on earth derives its name." This means there is only one family here on earth and in heaven, we are one. There is one family in heaven and earth. If we are walking in the realm of the Spirit—we will be in tuned with our family in heaven. Therefore we can hear their music and write their songs.

Also, the English Standard version says, "And I heard a voice from heaven like the roar of many waters and like the sound of loud thunder. The voice I heard was like the sound of harpists playing on their harps" (Revelation 14:2). When I realized the music was coming from heaven, I just relaxed and listened to the music.

Who Clawed Me in My Sleep?

I had another strange incident happen to me. I woke up in the middle of the night to a pain coming from the left side of my chest. I sat up and turned on the light to see what was causing the pain. There were five long, deep marks from something with very sharp claws on the left side of my chest. The area had already turned a dark red and was surrounded by thick scabs. My first thought was that I had been attacked by a demon. I pushed that thought from my mind as I tried to convince myself that my cat had clawed me.

When David saw the marks the next day, he asked me what had happened. I told him that the cat had clawed me. He looked at me like I was crazy! "That was no cat," he said. "The marks look like they came from a person who has long sharp nails with wide fingers. A cat cannot spread his claws that far apart."

It really hit me that if a cat cannot spread his claws that far apart, then it must have been a demon as I had first thought. I am always seeing a vision in my mind of the fingers and nails. It actually haunts me! I see the fingers as being very thin and the nails as being very long. I also can picture the ends of the nails that are very pointed and sharp.

I told my husband that I felt it was a demon. To this day, he refuses to discuss it with me. I know he blocks it out of his mind with no intention of ever bringing it up again. Deep down, I believe that he knows it was a demon. I do not believe he would ever admit it to anyone. When I first looked at the marks, they looked as if they had been healing for a couple of weeks; the scabs were pretty thick. At the time, I never thought to take a picture of the marks, but now I wish I had pictures to share.

I truly believe that, after the demon attacked me, an angel came and started a healing process. That same night I was attacked, I fell into a deep sleep and was taken somewhere. I didn't know where I was! I saw my sister who had died from breast cancer seven years earlier. I saw her from a distance and she saw me. It felt as if I was floating toward her. I remember touching her shoulder with my left hand. There was such a deep love that was transferred to me from her. It was so overwhelming—it was a love that was not from this world. Never in my life had I experienced such a strong healing type of love. It was like I was in a different dimension. Through this experience, I learned that the love I have on earth is just a touch compared to the love I felt with my sister in this heavenly encounter. I feel it was the same heavenly love that we will encounter with Jesus Christ when we see Him face to face. It made me feel safe, complete, and fulfilled. I had not a care in the world. It was as if God's arms were wrapped around me for eternity. That is a pretty potent experience of love. I'm sure that the next time I experience that kind of love, I will be in heaven!

I Received a Bookmark from an Angel

I was going through a lot of hard times when I decided to ask the Lord for His help. I decided to ask the Lord if I could see one more angel. I was working at a fast food drive-through. While I was working, a guy drove up to the window to get his order. He paid and then pulled ahead a little farther than he should have. It was as if he did not want me to get a good look at his face. He had blond hair, an average build, and was nice-looking. His blue ski jacket was very noisy. He talked very calmly and softly. He kept on asking me to take a bookmark from his hand. He was very insistent that I take the bookmark. I refused several times, but he was very persistent. Finally, he said, "Just take it and give it to a friend."

I realized that the entire time he had been talking to me, not one car had come to the drive-through—it was as if time had stood still. I took the bookmark and thanked him. He drove up a bit and I turned away from him. As my hand touched the bookmark, I could feel a presence come over me. In my spirit, I knew he was an angel—and I knew in my heart that it was true! The cars started coming through the drive-through again and I realized that there had been a pause in time. I looked at both sides of the bookmark. I got a strong urge to take another look at him. I looked at his rear-view mirror and saw a half-smile like I'd never seen before. It was as if he had accomplished his duty. The smile seemed not from this world. It was a smile I could never explain in words.

I still have the bookmark—I will never lose it! I was going through some problems and it was something I really needed. The bookmark said, "God's Twelve-Step Program for Dealing with Grief." It had no trademark or author's name. I have been looking all over to see if I could find that kind of bookmark, but I have not found one like it. I know that the bookmark came from an angel. I believe that the bookmark is not from this earth!

There are very few people who know these stories. I knew that most people would have a hard time believing. I began to think that, if God loved me enough to send me these angels to minister to my grief and pain, then maybe if I shared these stories with you, it would bring you faith, hope, and love in place of your grief and pain.

God says, "And now abide faith, hope, and love, these three; but the greatest of these is love" (I Corinthians 13:13). Receiving love from other believers around us can help us soften our heart to the point that we can receive Jesus Christ and respond to Him.

"For God so loved the world, that he gave his only begotten Son, that whosoever believeth in him should not perish, but have everlasting life" (John 3:16). He gave His life for you that you may enjoy eternity with him forever. There will be a day with no more sorrow, no more pain, and no more tears. To enjoy eternity with Jesus, all you have to do is accept his free gift of salvation, and the blood He shed for you on Calvary. Admit that you're a sinner and ask Him to come into your heart and make Him Lord and Savior of your life.

God's

12 Step Program for Dealing with Grief

1) There is no right or wrong way to grieve
-John 11:33-35

2) Deal with it one hour at a time
-Matthew 6:34

3) Talk about it
-John 14:1

4) Join a group of others who are grieving
-Ephesians 5:19

5) Stay close to believing friends
-Job 6:14

6) It's okay to ask why
-Proverbs 3:5-6

7) Take care of yourself
-Psalm 23

8) Keep busy
-Psalm 138:8

9) Don't let your heart be troubled
-John 14:1-4

10) Record your thoughts in a journal
-Psalm 147:3

11) Turn your grief into creative energy
-1 Thessalonians 5:14

12) Tap into your faith
-Deuteronomy 31:6

God's

12 Step Program for Dealing with Grief

1) Take time to cry

2) Don't let yourself get overwhelmed

3) Share your grief

4) Make uplifting friends who have been through your experience

5) Your friends will be there for you

6) You will understand someday

7) Your life is valuable

8) Do purposeful work that occupies your mind

9) You did the best you could at the time

10) Help get your feelings out

11) Find a way to help others

12) God is waiting with open arms

Chapter 2

Bondage of Legalism

Laws and Traditions

In many different beliefs, people think that they can earn their salvation by keeping different man-made laws or traditions. They think that if they don't keep these laws or traditions, they will lose their salvation. They feel like they have to do these certain things to earn their salvation. If they cannot keep the level of these standards, they feel like they have failed both God and man. They are always questioning whether or not they are going to make it to heaven. They wonder constantly if they are saved or not saved—or if God still loves them or not. This starts to produce heavy guilt and self-condemnation by not keeping the laws or traditions of men. Some begin to lose hope and go back to the ways of the world. They feel more accepted there instead of living with the constant feeling of failure and condemnation because they can't keep the Old Testament laws and traditions of men.

Whenever I am talking to someone who has given up, I want to let them know that there is good news for them! The Old Testament law was meant to show us that we are all sinners in need of a Savior. The Word of God talks about living for Jesus—free of the bondage of guilt and condemnation!

Righteousness That Equals the Law

Romans 3:21-23 says, "But now the righteousness of God without the law is manifested, being witnessed by the law and the prophets; Even the righteousness of God which is by faith of Jesus Christ unto all and upon all them that believe: for there is no difference [distinction]: For all have sinned, and come [fall] short of the glory of God."

The first part of this scripture says, "But now the righteous of God without the law is manifested." I asked someone a simple question: "What do you have to do to go to heaven?" They responded, "Be a good person, live a moral life, keep the Ten Commandments, be faithful to your spouse and several other things." I said, "Do you know what you have to do to go to heaven? You would have to have a righteousness that equals God's righteousness." They replied, "What! There is no one that has a righteousness that equals God's. Only one man did and that was Jesus Christ." I said, "You're right! None of us has ever kept the law or commandments perfectly, but we do need a righteousness that equals God's in order to be accepted before Him into Heaven." The kind of righteousness that God offers us is a righteousness that is "by faith in Jesus Christ, unto all and upon all them that believe . . ." There are two kinds of righteousness—the righteousness of man and the righteousness of God.

The righteousness of man is the very best that he can possibly be—the good works he does—but this will not make you acceptable before God. You need to have a righteousness that's equal to God's. The righteousness of God is God's own righteousness. It is His acceptance of us based on our belief in what Jesus provided through His death on the cross: forgiveness of sins and imputing to us a righteousness that equals the law. "For if by one man's offense, death reigned by one [Adam]; much more they which receive abundance of grace and of the gift of righteousness shall reign in life by one, Jesus Christ" (Romans 5:17). "Now it was not written for his [Abraham's] sake alone, that it was imputed [accepted and approved] to him; But for us also, to whom it shall be imputed [accepted and approved], if we believe on Him that raised up Jesus our Lord from the dead; Who was delivered for our offenses, and was raised again for our justification" (Romans 4:23-25).

God offers a *gift* of righteousness (right standing before God) made available freely to us through Jesus Christ.

Who are the Pharisees?

The Apostle Paul describes the Pharisees as very strict in following the laws that they could not keep them themselves. They did demand everyone else to keep every one of them. These Pharisees said long prayers, wore long robes, put on godly outward appearances to display their righteousness, and despised those who didn't live up to their standards.

Religious traditions are handed down from generation to generation. We must be careful that we do not twist scriptures to pervert the Gospel. It's important not to take one verse out of context. Read the previous chapter and the verse after to get the true meaning of what is being said in totality.

Different beliefs have convinced many people that you have to do many things to keep your salvation. So much lack of truth is caused by not knowing the Bible. People trust and believe what others are saying is true. The Bible says, "Work out your own salvation with fear and trembling; for it is God who is at work in you, both to will and to work His good pleasure" (Philippians 2:12-13). We need to search out the scriptures ourselves to see what's true.

Biblical holiness does not have a hardness of heart, legalism, or mean-spirited people making everyone miserable with their own list of man-made standards. Being holy is not rules and regulations that you are taught through the traditions of men; holiness is acquired when we receive the Holy Spirit. Jesus Christ in us is what makes us holy. Colossians 2:8-23 says, "Don't let others spoil your faith and joy with their philosophies, their wrong and shallow answers built on men's thoughts and ideas. Instead of on what Christ has said?"

In Biblical Days

In the bible, people had many traditions, such as washing of the hands, fasting, and keeping holy the Sabbath day. Women were not even allowed to speak in churches in those days. They were considered lower than a man and were treated very badly.

Even in the Old Testament, there were customs that were not from God. They believed that these customs were from God; many were taught to them as children. All through the generations, mankind has had customs and standards. Sometimes men would get together and agree on something that would become a law. Certain foolish standards would become a law; if it was not kept, it was called sin. If you did not obey, you would be in sin! Sin, according to the law, and you would be stoned to death. They watched others struggle to obey the laws that they had come up with! They would feel a higher power—and then pride would set in. They believed that they were better than everyone else by keeping these laws. The Bible says, "There is a way that seems right to a man, but its end is the way to death" (Proverbs 16:25). Traditions of men are hard to break. They have been handed down from generation to generation.

> "And he spake this parable unto certain which trusted in themselves that they were righteous, and despised others: Two men went up into the temple to pray; the one a Pharisee, and the other a publican. The Pharisee stood and

prayed thus with himself, God, I thank thee, that I am not as other men are, extortioners, unjust, adulterers, or even as this publican. I fast twice in the week; I give tithes of all I possess. And the publican, standing afar off, would not lift up so much as his eyes unto heaven, but smote upon his breast saying, God be merciful to me a sinner. I tell you, this man went down to his house justified rather than the other: for every one that exalted himself shall be abased; and he that humbleth himself shall be exalted" (Luke 18:9-14).

Some people who are brought up in certain traditions think that they have the truth so there is no need to look any further. Instead, the Bible admonishes them to "study to show thyself approved unto God a workmen that needed not to be ashamed, rightly dividing the word of truth" (II Timothy 2:15). Instead of studying scriptures, they look at everyone else as deceived. This may have been taught to them as children—or they have not studied the scriptures. Some people in America look at other nations and wonder how they can believe their customs and/or traditions. However, in America, we have a lot of our own customs and traditions. People are brought up in a certain belief and blindness sets in—they believe that they have the truth. The Bible says, "Can the blind lead the blind? Will they not both fall into the ditch?" (Luke 6:39).

The Grace of God

Grace—the Greek word Charis—means "the free, unmerited, undeserved favor of God." It is given to those who actually deserve the opposite and cannot be earned by works. Charisma is translated by the word "gift" or "free gift," especially emphasizing that it is of grace. Charisma is a specific form or manifestation of God's grace. John 1:17 says, "For the law was given through Moses, but grace and truth came through Jesus Christ." Grace can only be received by the humble. God resisted the proud, but giveth grace unto the humble. Salvation comes from the Greek word sozo, meaning "saved, healed, delivered, and prospered." Salvation is a free gift—you can't earn it and nothing you do can save you. Only what Jesus Christ did for you when He shed His blood for you on Calvary can save you. If you add or take away anything from your salvation, you are telling God that the blood He shed for you was not good enough. "God paid a ransom to save you from the impossible road to heaven which your fathers tried to take, and the ransom He paid was not mere gold or silver, as you very well know. But He paid for you with the precious life blood of Christ, the sinless, spotless, Lamb of God" (Peter 1:18-19).

Believe in Jesus and accept who He is and what He has done for you! Every belief in the world will tell you things that you have to do to go to Heaven. True Christianity is the only one in the world that tells you that Jesus Christ did it all for you! Legalism has been replaced by the grace of God!

Chapter 3

Who Are They?

The Hybrid of Fallen Angels

Many people have never heard of the giants before, but they are spoken of in the Bible. They lived in human form. Fallen angels were also called the giants. They were the hybrid of fallen angels who were very tall and powerful; they were also called the "mighty men." The giants had sex with the earthly women, which made the whole world corrupt, with all the people very evil within their hearts and very violent in those days. To me, they sound kind of like aliens!

Who were the giants in the Bible? "Now a population explosion took place upon the earth. It was at this time that the beings from the spirit world looked upon the beautiful earth women and took any they desired to be their wives. Then Jehovah said, 'My spirit must not forever be disgraced in man, wholly evil as he is. I will give him 120 years to mend his ways'" (Genesis 6:1-4). In those days, and even afterward, when the evil beings from the spirit world were sexually involved with human women, their children became giants of whom so many legends are told.

Demons are unclean; many people are possessed and are influenced by them! Demons are spirits that can also appear in a human form. Demons can roam through outer space and different dimensions. This scripture talks about the warring of angels going against the Prince of Darkness. Gabriel had to go and deliver a message:

Then he said, "Don't be afraid, Daniel. Since the first day you began to pray for understanding and to humble yourself before your God, your request has been heard in heaven. I have come in answer to your prayer. But for twenty-one days, the spirit prince of the kingdom of Persia blocked my way.

Then Michael, one of the archangels, came to help me, and I left him there with the spirit prince of the kingdom of Persia. Now I am here to explain what will happen to your people in the future, for this vision concerns a time yet to come" (Daniel 10:12-14).

Here is a scripture of an evil spirit that was in a body:

"They went across the lake to the region of the Gerasene. When Jesus got out of the boat, a man with an evil spirit came from the tombs to meet Him. This man lived in the tombs, and no one could bind him anymore, not even with a chain. For he had often been chained hand and foot, but he tore the chains apart and broke the irons on his feet. No one was strong enough to subdue him. Night and day among the tombs and in the hills he would cry out and cut himself with stones" (Mark 5:1-5).

Do Ghosts Really Haunt Houses?

Some ghosts might seem to be good, but there is always something behind it. They will never do things for your good! Humans cannot turn into ghosts; they are spirits, after they die. Lots of people say that the people who die can't leave this earth for some unsolved business. Hebrew 9:27 says, "Just as man is destined to die once, and after that to face judgment." Demons can impersonate a person. Demons can turn themselves into people—just like the good angels of God can. "And no wonder, for Satan himself masquerades as an angel of light. It is not surprising, then, if his servants masquerade as servants of righteousness. Their end will be what their actions deserve" (2 Corinthians 11:14-15).

The demons can even impersonate voices; they know your weaknesses. Some ghosts might seem to be good, but there is always a reason behind it. The main reason that they want you to seek them and believe in them is so they can get your mind off of God—so you can trust in someone else besides Jesus!

Demons can be in physical or spirit form when they are allowed to roam the earth. People who are deceased cannot stay on earth and haunt the living. In the scriptures, there isn't any in-between.

> "The time came when the beggar died and the angels carried him to Abraham's side. The rich man also died and was buried. In hell where he was in torment, he looked up and saw Abraham

far away, with Lazarus by his side. So he called to him, "Father Abraham, have pity on me and send Lazarus to dip the tip of his finger in water and cool my tongue, because I am in agony in this fire" (Luke 16:22-24).

Hebrew 9:27 says, "Just as man is destined to die once, and after that to face judgment."

Chapter 4

The Spirit World

Put on All of God's Armor!

We have a tremendous amount of influence going on in the spirit world. There is supernatural warfare going on around us. The spiritual warfare is invisible. Angels and demons are fighting in our minds and in the things we do. In the spiritual warfare, the battle is on! Good angels are fighting with us to get us into heaven. The demons are doing everything to get us into hell! Demons are going to hell—and they want our company.

We need to trust in His word; we need Jesus. We need to put on the whole armor of God!

"Put on all of God's armor so that you will be able to stand safe against all strategies and tricks of Satan. For we are not fighting against people made of flesh and blood, but against persons without bodies—the evil rulers of the unseen world, those mighty satanic beings and great evil princes of darkness who rule this world—and against huge numbers of wicked spirits in the spirit world. Use every piece of God's armor to resist the enemy whenever he attacks, and when it is all over, you will still be standing up. But to do this, you will need the strong belt of truth and the breastplate of God's approval. Wear shoes that are able to speed you on as you preach the Good News of peace with God. In every battle, you will need faith as your shield to stop the fiery arrows aimed at you by Satan—and you will need the helmet of salvation and the sword of the Spirit, which is the Word of God" (Ephesians 6:11-17).

Isaiah 14:12-14 says, "How you have fallen from heaven, O morning star, son of the dawn! You have been cast down to the earth, you who once laid low the nations! You said in your heart, 'I will ascend to heaven; I will raise my throne above the stars of God; I will sit enthroned on the mount of assembly. On the utmost heights of the sacred mountain. I will ascend above the tops of the clouds; I will make myself like the Most High."

"Dear friends, do not believe every spirit, but test the spirits whether they are of God, because many false prophets have gone out into the world. This is how you can recognize the Spirit of God: Every spirit that acknowledges that Jesus Christ has come in the flesh is from God, but every spirit that does not acknowledge Jesus is not from God. This is the spirit of the Antichrist, which you have heard is coming and even now is already in the world. You, dear children, are from God and have overcome them, because the one who is in you is greater than the one who is in the world" (1 John 4:1-4).

Chapter 5

My Poems

God Wants to Take You Home

We are just visiting; we are not here to stay.
This life is a test; we need to pray.
We have to realize we are only here for a short while.
This life we live in is just a trial.
There are messengers telling people, "Keep your faith."
Soon we will be home.
There are so many people who are slaves of Satan.
They just want to roam.
In the world there is so much sorrow, so much pain.
The outsiders say God is to blame.
Did you know that God owns your soul? He owns you.
He knows your heart, your thoughts, and everything
    you do.
The unfaithful will be doomed in the lake of fire for
    eternity.
They had their own chance with their own personality.
For the faithful ones, He will give everything to you.

So don't worry about the material things; don't be so blue.

Just believe in Jesus, for He is your best friend.

Heaven is so beautiful, you cannot comprehend.

People need to realize how to be saved.

Believe in Jesus, and you are on your way.

You are ashamed of the Lord while He is crying for you.

When Judgment Day comes, He'll be ashamed of you too.

Two spirits want you—God and Satan.

If you don't pick God, guess who will be waiting.

If Satan's got you fooled, God will be blue.

God will dwell on you, then spit you out and forget you.

You'll be thrown into hell, wishing you were never born.

It will be too late; in the lake of fire you will mourn.

Satan is laughing as he has you conned.

Jumping up and down with his victory, he has won!

So a few years from now, where will you be?

It is your choice; you are free!

Will you be in heaven or hell, for all eternity?

You may think that this letter is a fairy tale and untrue.

That's what Satan wants you to think—the joke is on you!

The Last Generation

All we hear is "peace, peace" as the days go by.
Millions of people starving, people wondering why.
Distress and rebellion in all the nations we see.
God's judgment has come upon all of us
So people would repent and be set free.
One day soon, we shall be changed in a moment,
You will leave this earth in a flash in a twinkling of an
    eye.
So prepare yourself, for when that moment comes,
You will not even get a chance to say good-bye.
First the dead, then the righteous shall meet Him in the
    air
Then we will be with the Lord forever on that glorious
    day.
So be watchful, and don't forget to pray.
When He comes to take you home, it will be just
Like a normal day.
He will come like a thief in the night; He is on His way.
The signing of the Arab-Israel peace treaty,
Could it be the key?
For the covenant the Antichrist shall confirm,
Could it be?
Scriptures being prophesied, signs are being fulfilled.
Even the Jews' temple is being prepared to be rebuilt.
There will be a Great Tribulation,
One-World government it shall be.
But during the last three and a half years,
God will pour out His wrath on the ungodly.

Jesus is coming back; we feel it in the air.
Even the Jews are going back to their homeland.
What a glorious time we live in when you know
All things are in God's hands.
In the last half of the tribulation there will be,
A blood-bath, you will see.
The blessed ones will be in heaven having a marriage
    supper
Happy as can be.
After the marriage supper, we'll go to the millennial,
What a glorious place.
We will be kings and priests ruling over every race.
After the kingdom's age is over, we'll go to heaven,
We will be in heaven for all eternity.
So don't worry about your past or your future,
Just put all your trust in the Lord who set you free!

Feel the Pain of Hell and the Joy of Heaven

Thrown into a pit, screaming, fire is hot and burning.
Worms and bugs all over your body, they will not stop
    crawling.

Gnashing of teeth, darkness you shall see.
Flames of fire burning for eternity!

Wailing and weeping in a fire of punishment.
You will be burning in a lake of fire, everlasting
    torment.

No rest day or night in the flame.
If you do not know Jesus, you will be to blame!

If you just think you are going to die and go in the
    ground.
I will be in heaven and won't be seeing you around.

I will be in heaven in a beautiful place.
I will run to His throne and see His face.

Flowers will be dancing.
Birds and angels will be singing.

The streets of the city will be pure gold.
Heaven will have jeweled walls, pearly gates as it was
    foretold!

Chapter 6

My Family's Stories

My Mom and Dad Saw an Angel

This is the story of the experience my mom and dad had in their two-story second home. They had their sixteen-year-old grandson with them for the weekend and were sitting in the upper level of the house where the kitchen and living room are located. From the living room window, they could clearly see their seven and a half acres of wooded land. My mom and dad were sitting in the living room by the big window. Travis said that he was going to cut some branches off a tree in the woods. They were watching to make sure he was safe. He was on a four-wheeler about 150 feet from the house. He stopped by the tree that he was gonna cut the branches from.

As my parents were watching through the window, my dad said to my mom, "Look, someone is coming out of the woods!" It was a young man who looked to be the same age as Travis. He was walking toward Travis. My mom asked who the young man was and where had he come from. My dad did not know. There weren't any houses in that direction. The young man walked up to Travis. They noticed that he was wearing the same kind of clothing—and even the same kind of cap. He was identical to Travis. They could not see his face very clearly because he was facing the opposite direction. She asked my dad if she should walk outside to see who the kid was. Dad said, "He will be okay, we'll just watch."

As Travis was using the chainsaw, the young man stayed right next to him. He was moving his body back and forth as if he was helping Travis. This continued for around fifteen minutes as my mom and dad kept watching closely. My dad said, "It looks like he's helping Travis with the chainsaw." Suddenly, the young man walked halfway into Travis's body—and then he vanished! As they watched him disappear, Travis's body was lit up like a neon light.

Travis rode the four-wheeler back toward the house, but as soon as he arrived at the house, the neon light disappeared. As he entered the house, Travis complained that there was something in his eye. My mother went to get him a washcloth and asked, "Who was that young man helping you?" Travis said, "Nobody was with me." She said, "Grandpa and I watched you the whole time with that young man—so we saw everything! Who was with you, Travis?"

Travis repeatedly told her that there was no one with him. Mom knew in her spirit that she had seen an angel. Dad also believed that he had seen an angel. She knew from the Lord that the angel was there to protect Travis. They had seen the angel rocking back and forth as if he was holding something down. It looked as if he was holding down the chainsaw blade from jolting back toward Travis. They felt that the angel came to save Travis's life or to protect him from a serious chainsaw accident. My mom and dad only told a few people the story because it would be hard for anyone to believe. They knew it was true because both of them had seen the same thing happen at the same time. They both thanked the Lord Jesus that He had protected their treasured grandson.

My Sister Saw a Vision

In December 2002, our sister passed away from breast cancer; she was only forty-one years old. It was very hard for the whole family—as it would be for any family. She was in the prime of her life, had a loving husband, and four beautiful children.

After my sister passed away, my other sister was in bed when a vision came upon her. She had seen my sister completely still on the bed—and then she saw her coming out of her dead body. She was so beautiful. She was wearing a white gown and kept rising out of her dead body, glowing all over. She looked so happy and beautiful; her hair was all curled and her face was picture-perfect.

My sister believes that this vision is worth a thousand words. As she rose to the ceiling, she eventually disappeared. She could tell that she was once again complete and literally in good spirits. She was whole again—and was going to meet her maker. This gave her peace; she was no longer in pain—and she would never feel pain again. Praise the Lord for everlasting life in a wonderful new body where there is no more suffering or pain—just happily ever after.

She knew that this came from the Lord to give her—and our family—peace. As she was having this vision, she could feel the Holy Spirit come upon her. In your deepest trials, the Lord will be with you to comfort you. Ask and you shall be answered.

This is a letter that my sister wrote to my mom and dad right after her vision. This is typed out exactly the way it was written. The real letter is shown after this one—in case the real letter is too hard to see.

Dec 26, 2002

Dear Mom and Dad,

I just want to thank you both for the wonderful visit I had with the both of you. And I would just like to say you both look great. I was very glad to see that you both had a peace that only the Lord can give you when something like this occurs. It is a pain that parents are never suppose to go through and few parents that do lose a child, in general, children are suppose to go after the parents and not before. But as we all know, God has a reason for everything and His ways are the right ways. We only see a very small picture and sometimes we can't even see the small picture very clearly but God does have the big picture totally in control. Praise the Lord for that.

I cannot put into words the loss we will all be feeling for quite some time. We will feel at peace some days with this and other days we will even question why God had to take Sue at such an early age of 41. With us being human this is natural and I can't tell you it will be easy but with the Lord it certainly can be easier. And all we have to do is ask. God can and He will give us peace and comfort when we ask. Now that is a loving God.

Mom and dad I felt I needed to write you both because of the peace God has given me about Sue. We talked about it at our visit and now I want to write it down on paper so <u>mom</u> you can read it over and over because I do know you need to hear it. I want you to know and I also want you to have assurance that Sue is now in heaven and she is healed. Sue accepted Jesus Christ as her personal Savior years ago and her walk showed it. Once again for a few years you only seen a very small picture of what Sue was like but at her funeral I do believe you seen her full picture, what she was actually about. None of us are perfect, therefore none of us by <u>our</u> righteousness could make it to heaven but thanks be to God that He sent His only son to bare our unrighteousness and to replace it with <u>His</u> righteousness. When we come to Christ, He cleans us with His blood that He shed on Calvary and makes us in right standing with Him. Isn't that wonderful and this is the Greatest Gospel ever told and the only story that has never changed.

When I was called to see my counselor on Dec 18th I really did not expect to hear the news that I had heard. I walked into Mr. Siler's office and I believe his words were "You have been expecting this" and I then knew what he was talking about. I then said "It is my sister Sue, she died didn't she." And he shook his head yes. I felt tears running down my face. Even though I knew in the back of my mind Sue was not doing good I still prayed daily for Sue and I had hope that she would pull through. When you have a loved one that is ill you always want to believe the best. I was shocked but yet I could feel the comfort that the Lord was giving me. I then called the both of you and I really sensed you were both being comforted with the Lord also. (In times like this I do not understand how a non-Christian could ever go through a trial like that alone). So after I hung the phone up God really gave me a peace about it, and this is what I visualized in my mind. I seen Sue laying in bed and when she took her last breath her spirit came out of her (with her spirit being perfect without illness or suffering) and she looked down at her body and she looked up to heaven and got a taste of her eternal life and she ran toward her Savior. She is up in heaven now and you remember her laugh and her smile that she always wore. She once again has it on her face again and it will never be taken away from her like it was down here.

It says in the Word that we should be sad when a baby is born and happy when a person dies. This world is just the opposite. We should be sad when a baby is born because of the evil world it is and when a person dies, such as Sue, who was saved will go to heaven and spend eternity with our loving Lord.

Sue would not want her mom and dad to be sad at the occasion of her being with the Lord. Although, we are human and in our flesh we will grieve. But please know Sue is in a much better place and she is "whole". I picture her up in heaven with her great smile and her wonderful laugh. I know she loved you both and we all will see her again. Please just know that Sue wants you both to be strong and with Sue being taken from us it is a trial in our lives. We need to now be happy for Sue, she is in heaven and she is healed from her sickness. Amen.

Where the highlight is, is what I basically wrote to Joe. I know you wanted it in writing and so now if you have any questions please write them down in a letter to me.

I love you both and I already miss you both and you just were here.

Love always,
Cathy

Dec 26, 2002

Dear mom and dad

I just want to thank you both for the wonderful visit I had with the both of you. And I would just like to say you both look great. I was very glad to see that you both had a peace that only the Lord can give you when something like this occurs. It is a pain that parents are never suppose to go through and few parents that do lose a child. In general, children are suppose to ~~pass~~ after the parents and not ~~before~~. But as ~~we~~ all know God has a reason for everything and His ways are the right ways. We only see a very small picture and sometimes we can't even see the small picture very clearly but God does have the big picture totally in control. Praise the Lord for that.

I can not put into words the loss we will all be feeling for quite some time. We will feel at peace some days with this and other days we will even question ~~why~~ God had to take Sue at such a early age of 41. With us being human this is natural and I can't tell you it will be easy but with the Lord it certainly can be easier. And all we have to do is ask. God can and He will give us peace and comfort when we ask. Wow that is a loving God.

Mom and dad I felt I needed to write you both because of the peace God has given me about Sue. We talked about it at our visit and now I want to write it down on paper so mom you can read it over and over because I do know you need to hear it. I want you to know and I also want you to have assurance that Sue is now in heaven and she is healed. Sue accepted Jesus Christ as her personal Savior years ago and her walk showed it. Once again for the two years you only seen a very small picture of what Sue was like but at her funeral I do believe you seen her full picture what she was actually about. None of us are perfect, therefore none of us by our righteousness could make it to heaven but thanks be to God that He sent His only son to bare our unrighteousness and to replace it with His righteousness. When we come to Christ He cleans us with His blood that He shed on Calvary and makes us in right standing with Him. Isn't that wonderful and this is the Greatest Gospel ever told and the only story that has never changed.

When I was called to see my counselor on Dec 18th I really did not expect to hear the news that I had heard. I walked into Mr. Miller's office and I believe his words were "You have been expecting this" and I then knew what he was talking about. I then said "She is my sister Sue, she died didn't she." And he shook his head yes. I felt tears running down my face. Even though I knew in the back of my mind Sue was not doing good, I still prayed daily for Sue and I had hope that she would pull through. When you have a loved one that is ill you always want to believe the best. I was shocked but yet I could feel the comfort that the Lord was giving me. I then called the both of you and I really sensed you were both being comforted with the Lord also (In times like this I do not understand how a non-christian could even go through a trial like that alone). So after I hung the phone up God really gave me a peace about it, and this is what I visualized in my mind. I seen Sue laying in bed and when she took her last breath her spirit came out of her (with her spirit being perfect without illness or suffering) and she looked down at her body and she looked up to heaven and got a taste of her eternal hope and she ran toward her Savior. She is up in heaven now and you remember her laugh and her smile that she always wore. She once again has it on her face again and it will never be taken away from her like it was down here.

It says in the Word that we should be sad when a baby is born and happy when a person dies. This world is great the opposite. We should be sad when a baby is born because of the evil world it is and when a person dies, such as Sue, who was saved will go to heaven and spend eternity with our loving Lord.

Sue would not want her mom and dad to be sad at the occasion of her being with the Lord. Although, we are human and in our flesh we will grieve. But please know Sue is in a much better place and she is "whole". I picture her up in heaven with her great smile and her wonderful laugh. I know she told you ~~this~~ and we all will see her again. Please just know that she wants you both to be strong and with Sue being taken from us it is a trial in our lives. We need to ~~be~~ now be happy for Sue, she is in heaven and she is healed from her sickness / Amen

When the ~~right time~~ is is what I briefly wrote to God. I know you wanted it in writing and so now if you have any questions ~~please~~ write them down in a letter to me.

I love you both and I already miss you both and you just were here.

Love
Always
Cathy

An Angel in the Woods

When my brother was a teenager, he hung out with one of his best friends, Gary. They did everything together. One of the things that they did was go to remote places just to hang out. One day, they decided to go to Butternut, which is in the northern part of Wisconsin. It was one of the biggest woods that they had ever experienced. For a couple of kids their age, it was so cool. When they got there, they started walking in the woods and kept on walking and walking the paths. Suddenly, they realized that they were deep in the woods. It was very secluded. My brother stopped in a certain area. While he looked around, Gary kept on walking. My brother realized that Gary was quite far ahead. All of a sudden, a guy came out of the woods from nowhere! This man started to talk about Jesus, and then he gave my brother a gospel tract. My brother started to look at the tract, and then realized that it was a tract on Jesus about how to get saved! When my brother looked up, the man was nowhere in sight. He soon realized how strange it was for someone in the middle of the deep woods to give him a gospel tract and talk about Jesus. Could it have been an angel?

The Sinner's Prayer

Jesus, I ask you to come into my heart and life. Cleanse me and make me a new person in you right now. I believe that you are the Son of God and that you died on the cross for me. Forgive me for all my sins.

Thank you for the blood you shed for me on Calvary that I might be saved. I receive you as my Lord and Savior.

In Jesus name, I pray. Amen.

Now that you have prayed this prayer, Corinthians 5:17 says, "Therefore, if anyone is in Christ, he is a new creation; old has gone, the new has come!" Friend, you have a whole new life with Jesus ahead of you. See you in heaven!

In this book I want to share with you some of my encounters that led me to my bookmark. My encounters and my bookmark are not the reasons that I wrote this book! I wrote this book because I was pressured by the Lord to write about breaking the bondage of legalism!

***It sounds like heavenly music and I can hear many people singing like a magnificent choir. I thought I was losing my mind and would use my hands to shake my head back and forth in an attempt to rid myself of this music.

***There were five long, deep marks from something with very sharp claws on the left side of my chest. The area had already turned a dark red and was surrounded by thick scabs. My first thought was that I had been attacked by a demon. I pushed that thought from my mind as I tried to convince myself that my cat had clawed me.

***I don't know where I was! I saw my sister who had died of breast cancer seven years earlier. I saw her from a distance and she saw me. It felt as if I was floating toward her. I remember touching her shoulder with my left hand. Then there was such a deep love that was transferred to me from her. It was so overwhelming—it was a love that was not from this world!

***I stared at the bookmark and then I looked at his rear-view mirror. I had a strong urge to take another look at him. When I did, I saw that he had a half smile like I'd never seen; it was as if he had just accomplished his duty. The smile was not from this world. It was a smile I could never explain in words.

My Bookmark is Inside the Book.
God's Twelve-Step Program for Dealing with Grief

Julie Ringer is a writer and a poet who lives with her husband in Wisconsin. She has a Pomeranian and a black cat. She always reads the Bible for hours each and every day. She learned very quickly not to trust her soul in anyone else's hands.